TaTe to TaTe

An Illustrated Walk along London's South Bank.

by tommy penton

With a Walking Companion by
Brian Parker.

Jonathan Cape . London

Published by Jonathan Cape 2008

2 4 6 8 10 9 7 5 3 1

Copyright © Tommy Penton 2008
Walking Companion © Brian Parker 2008

Tommy Penton has asserted his right under the Copyright, Designs
and Patents Act 1988 to be identified as the author of this work

First published in Great Britain in 2008 by
JONATHAN CAPE
Random House, 20 Vauxhall Bridge Road,
London SW1V 2SA

www.rbooks.co.uk

Addresses for companies within The Random House Group Limited
can be found at: www.randomhouse.co.uk/offices.htm

The Random House Group Limited Reg. No. 954009

A CIP catalogue record for this book is available from the British Library

ISBN 9780224085151

Printed and bound in China by C&C Offset Printing Co., Ltd

for Milly.

Walk
east →

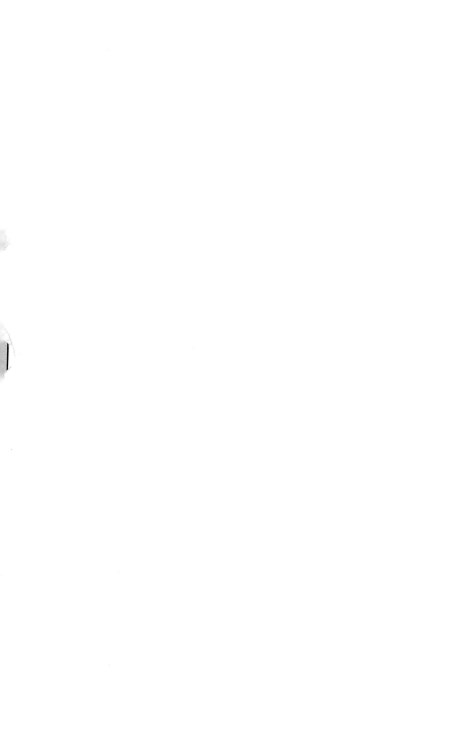

Walk
← West

A WALKING COMPANION

SCENE ONE

This scene of the opening walk looks downstream from **Albert Embankment** across the river towards **Vauxhall Bridge** and **Battersea Power Station**. On the left are the exotic, twisting-dolphin cast-iron lamp posts (1895), so characteristic of this part of the embankment. The yellow and red bridge is **Vauxhall Bridge**, built in 1895–1906 and embellished with bronze female figures representing the Arts and Sciences. They can just be seen, at the risk of vertigo, from the bridge walkway and must be more easily viewed from a boat on the river.

Over the bridge and identified by its four chimneys, is the Art-Deco **Battersea Power Station**. Our walk is also a walk from power station to power station, although the only connection that Battersea Power Station has with art was early concern at the effect of its fumes on the paintings in Tate Britain and the appearance of the building on the cover of the Pink Floyd album *Animals* in 1977. Both Battersea and Bankside (later the Tate Modern) involved the same architect, Sir Giles Gilbert Scott, who was also the architect of Liverpool Cathedral.

At Bankside we have a striking development success and at Battersea a series of development failures and a building without a function for twenty-four years. As the *Guardian* put it, 'loved but purposeless'. Battersea Power Station is the largest brick building in Europe and set the pattern for power-station design. Seen as an upside-down billiard table and compared once to Albi Cathedral, it has found a place in the hearts of Londoners, but its future is uncertain.

The green tower block to the right of Battersea Power Station is the **Panoramic Building** (1969–71), once the headquarters of Rank Hovis McDougall, leading UK flour millers. The building has now been converted to flats, reflecting a current trend in London of converting office space to residential. The other building is **Riverbank House** (1964–66), offices for the Regional Coordination Unit, which coordinates central government policy with the regions. In front of these offices sits 'Locking Piece', a sculpture by Henry Moore (1968) suggested by two pebbles that fit together like a puzzle.

The white terraces, very symmetrical, were constructed by that ambitious nineteenth-century builder Thomas Cubitt, the developer of Belgravia and Pimlico. In the corner terrace can be found the **Morpheth Arms**, a Victorian pub (1845) of cut glass and wood-panelled interiors originally built for the warders of nearby Millbank Penitentiary. The ghost of a prisoner is supposed to haunt the cellars.

This sector of the river is called **Millbank** and is named after the fourteenth-century Abbey Mill, which then belonged to Westminster Abbey. Between 1812 and 1821 Millbank Penitentiary, a huge prison of 1100 cells, was constructed on this site. The prison looked like a French chateau and had octagonal walls and a moat. It held prisoners awaiting transport to Van Diemen's Land (Tasmania) and Botany Bay (New South Wales). They were kept in holding cells until taken down the river to prison hulks for final departure. The prison was demolished in 1892–3 to make way for the Tate Gallery.

The grey building, partly hidden by trees, is the former Royal Army Medical College, now adapted by Allies & Morrison for **Chelsea College of Art and Design**.

On the right is the classical portico of the Tate Gallery (now **Tate Britain**), the gift of sugar magnate Sir Henry Tate and designed by Sidney R.J. Smith. The Tate Gallery opened in 1897 as the home of British Art. Later an international modern collection was added and transferred to Tate Modern in 2000. The handsome sculpture galleries were donated by Lord Duveen. They were designed and built in 1935–37 by a New Yorker, J. Russsell Pope, who was the architect of the Jefferson Memorial in Washington. The gallery has been enlivened by the addition of the postmodern-style **Clore Gallery** (1987), designed by James Stirling and Michael Wilford, which houses the J.M.W. Turner collection of paintings. Nine new galleries and a bookshop were added by John Miller & Partners in 2001 along with a new entrance by Allies & Morrison. The result has made for a much more consumer-friendly environment. The pretty restaurant has charm with a mural by Rex Whistler which is called 'The Expedition in Pursuit of Rare Meats'.

SCENE THREE

This scene shows the landing stage for the Tate to Tate boat, which every forty minutes provides an exhilarating journey from Tate Britain to Tate Modern via the London Eye and back again.

The tower on the right is the **Millbank Tower** (1960–3), one of London's early skyscrapers. Millbank Tower was built originally for Vickers by Ronald Ward to rival the Shell Building across the river. It was Labour Party Headquarters from 1995 to 2002.

Scene Four

The vast office blocks facing us are **Thames House** (1929–30) and **Nobel House** (1927–9). They are designed in an in-between-the-wars style known as neo-Imperial. They have been described as looking like 'sculpted cliffs'. Nobel House was built for Imperial Chemical Industries, and is now occupied by Ofgem, the power regulator. Since 1944 Thames House has been occupied by MI5, the government department responsible for internal security. They are conveniently close to their brothers and sisters at MI6 across the river in Vauxhall Cross.

Scene Five

This dense and multitudinous view is of **Lambeth Bridge**, which links Westminster to Lambeth and was opened by George V in 1932. Its design is neo-Imperial and it is decorated at each end with giant obelisks surmounted by pine cones, or possibly pineapples. Lambeth Bridge is painted red to match the colour of the benches in the House of Lords.

Scene Six

Along the tops of the trees are the roofs and towers of **No 7 Millbank**, Westminster House (1913–15), an Edwardian neo-Wren building and the offices of British-American Tobacco Co. until they moved downstream.

No 4 Millbank (1912–16) is the former offices of the Crown Agents, which was a government corporation, reflected in its coat of arms over the door. Crown Agents is now privatised and continues to provide international development services. The building was refurbished in 1989–91 with television studios and contains the Atrium restaurant, a favourite of politicians from across the street.

No 1 Millbank (1903–06), seen here only by the tips of its chimneys, was the headquarters of the Church Commissioners, who manage the assets of the Church of England.

In March 2007 the Commissioners moved to Church House. This building, with its eccentric facade, was designed by W.D. Caröe, a major figure in the Arts and Crafts movement.

Along the northern bankside is the **Victoria Embankment**, which runs from Westminster Bridge to Blackfriars Bridge, the imaginative creation of Sir Joseph Bazalgette. His idea was to create an embankment roadway and run the main sewers of the city underneath it, thus redirecting them from emptying into the nearby Thames to outlets in the east of London. The result offered a roadway that relieved congestion from the Strand, public gardens and walkways providing amenity for the citizens and a new course for the District and Circle line underground railway.

SCENE SEVEN

To the right of this scene is the magnificent **Palace of Westminster**, called a 'palace' because it is historically a royal palace. It is more popularly known by its function as the Houses of Parliament. Here we see **Victoria Tower**, the grandest of three towers, the others being Central Tower and the fairy-tale Clock Tower.

Over the top of the Houses of Parliament peep the twin towers of **Westminster Abbey**, designed in a plausibly medieval style by Nicholas Hawksmoor in the early eighteenth century.

The **Victoria Tower Gardens**, identified by the trees to the left of Victoria Tower, are known for the statues of 'The Burghers of Calais' by Rodin and Emmeline Pankhurst, the suffragette, by A.G. Walker. Also, in the centre of the gardens can be found the recently restored exotic memorial by Charles Buxton to his father, Sir T.F. Buxton, a slave-trade abolitionist.

The Houses of Parliament were the work of Sir Charles Barry, the Classicist architect, who was assisted in this Gothic Revival composition by Augustus W.N. Pugin. 'A vast hallucination like the Gothic Revival itself,' commented the idiosyncratic architectural buff Ian Nairn. The Houses of Parliament were built between 1835 to 1860 and were a successful response to a competition following a major fire in 1834. The Parliament building had to be Gothic or Tudor, possibly to harmonise with Westminster Abbey. The Classical layout was married to Gothic detailing which reflected the obsessions of the two architects, who worked in an amicable collaboration of two opposites. Barry concentrated on the exterior and Pugin on the interior decoration. The result was summed up by Pugin as 'All Grecian, sir. Tudor details on a classic body.' Barry was knighted and Pugin died insane at the age of forty. Only Westminster Hall, with its glorious hammer-beam roof, remains, of the original medieval buildings, truly Gothic.

Our scene shows a continuation of the facade of the Houses of Parliament to the **Big Ben** tower. Big Ben refers to the thirteen-ton bell within the tower. The bell is named after the Commissioner for Works at the time of construction, Sir Benjamin Hall.

Westminster Bridge appears with its Gothic Revival ornamentation and lamp standards. Sir Charles Barry was involved in its design. The bridge opened in 1862 and is painted green, to reflect the colours of the House of Commons benches. There is an excellent view upstream which was immortalised in William Wordsworth's sonnet 'Composed upon Westminster Bridge, September 3, 1802', with its opening line 'Earth has not anything to show more fair'.

Of course, the scene has changed, but not the glorious effect.

On the left is the dark, contentious shape of **Portcullis House** (1998–2001), a no-expense-spared office block for Members of Parliament. The building was designed by Michael Hopkins and is linked by a subway to the Houses of Parliament. The black vent flues along the roof give out a contradictory message of Tudor palace and Victorian factory. The building sits atop the extraordinary, raw concrete, Piranesi-like Westminster Tube Station.

Just in front of Portcullis House is the **statue of Boadicea** with her daughters and vigorous horses pulling her scythe-wheeled chariot. Boadicea, Queen of the Iceni, led a revolt against the Romans in AD 61–63. The only time that London was ever destroyed was by Boadicea, ironically a Briton.

In the centre frame are the two blocks, in Scottish Baronial style by Norman Shaw, that form **New Scotland Yard**. The first block was built in 1888–90 and the south annex was added in 1902–06. These buildings were known as the 'jam factory' because of their horizontal bands of alternating red brick and Portland stone. New Scotland Yard was the headquarters of the Metropolitan Police from 1890 to 1967 and is now used by Members of Parliament as offices. This was originally the site of a medieval palace where Scottish kings stayed on visits to London.

Edging into the right of this scene

are the glass capsules of the **London Eye** (1993–2000), which is, by far, the most successful of the Millennium projects.

The Eye appears as a great rotating bicycle wheel and was designed by David Marks and Julia Barfield with engineering support from Arup and Associates. Financial support came from British Airways. Initially a contentious project, it is now a spectacular success, giving superb views of the city from each of its thirty-two capsules, which rotate for some thirty-five minutes. The Eye reaches a height equal to that of the spire of Salisbury Cathedral.

In the background is the bleak Kafkaesque **Ministry of Defence** (1939–59), which stands over the original Whitehall Palace wine cellars of Cardinal Wolsey.

The trees cover the **Victoria Embankment Gardens**, which were laid out on land reclaimed from the river. We can see **Whitehall Court** (1886–92), whose French Renaissance roofs seem to dance along the treetops. H.G. Wells and George Bernard Shaw once lived here. The edifice continues to the **National Liberal Club**, which shares the site with the **Royal Horse Guards Hotel**. This building can be identified by its upright corner tower. The brown building on the right is the **Metropole** building, which was formerly a nineteenth-century hotel, the Metropole.

The vessels moored here are the *Tattershall Castle*, a passenger-ferry steamer, built in 1934 for use on the River Humber, and *R.S. Hispaniola*, the former *Maid of Ashton*, which was launched in 1953 and employed as a passenger ferry around the west coast of Scotland. Now both offer a restaurant, bar and function rooms.

To the left is **Hungerford Bridge** (1864). This Victorian railway bridge was an eyesore and had replaced the elegant suspension bridge by Brunel. Now it has returned to elegance with the design of Lifschutz and Davidson's 'Golden Jubilee Bridges' in 2002. They attached two spectacular pedestrian walkways to the existing bridge. The concrete bridge decks are suspended on outward leaning pylons described by the architects as 'angels' wings'. The walkways provide access to the South Bank from Charing Cross Station and Surrey Pier.

Hidden behind the bridge is a spectacular postmodern office block called **Embankment Place**, designed by Terry Farrell and incorporating, under its wide curved roof, **Charing Cross Station**.

SCENE FOURTEEN

A continuation of the Hungerford Bridge and the right-hand-side walkway. The Edwardian kiosk with turret tower is now **Motions Bar and Club**.

In the Embankment Gardens can be found the **York Water Gate**, which dates back to 1626, then giving access to York House, the home of the Duke of Buckingham, the favourite of Charles I. This is a reminder that all along this part of the river were the houses of the mighty. They were occupied by bishops from the twelfth century to the Dissolution of the Monasteries. Then, as fortune changed, the nobility took their place and lived, overlooking the river, in such palaces as Somerset House, Essex House and Arundel House.

Unseen, just by the river, is a gilt-bronze eagle atop a pylon. This is the RAF Memorial (1921–3) by Sir Reginald Blomfield.

SCENE FIFTEEN

The 1930s Art-Deco **Adelphi** office block, with its cheery flags, is first seen on the left. It brutally replaced the magnificent Classical Revival Adephi Terrace of the Adams brothers, despite outrage at the time. Some elements of the original Adelphi remain, however, such as Nos 1–3 Robert Street. 'Adelphi' was chosen as it is the Greek word for 'brothers' (Robert, John and James). The Adelphi Terrace of set-back brick residences over warehouses was designed in the style of the palace of the Roman Emperor Diocletian at Spalato (Split), which Robert Adam had visited. Here lived David Garrick, Richard D'Oyley Carte and John Galsworthy. The development nearly bankrupted Robert Adam.

Next to the Adelphi office block a view of the **Telecom Tower** (1963–66) can be seen in the distance. It had a revolving restaurant at its top until bombed by the IRA in 1971. The tower is still used for broadcasting purposes.

Next is **Cleopatra's Needle** with its two sphinxes sitting on either side. The 186 ton obelisk originated in Aswan, Egypt, circa 1475 B.C. It was presented to the British in 1819 by Mohammed Ali, Viceroy of Egypt under the Ottoman Empire. It was erected in 1877 and its twin has been in Central Park, New York, since 1869.

Shell-Mex House with its characteristic eccentric clock face was built in 1886 as the Cecil Hotel. It was named after the Earls of Salisbury and was the largest hotel in Europe. Shell purchased the building in 1930 and remodelled the river facade in Art-Deco style. The clock was called 'Big Benzene'. It has been compared to a gigantic mantelpiece ornament.

The building on the right is the white-glazed terracotta **Savoy Hotel**, one of London's most famous hotels. Its river frontage was designed by Arthur Mackmurdo (1899). The hotel was financed by the profits of the impresario Richard D'Oyley Carte from performances of the Gilbert and Sullivan operas. The chef was Auguste Escoffier. Oscar Wilde dallied here with Lord Alfred Douglas, Monet used to lunch and dine here, and Fred Astaire and his sister danced here. Not all at the same time.

SCENE SIXTEEN

The steamer with twin funnels is the *Queen Mary*, built on the Clyde in 1933 and now offering 'the best fish and chips in London'.

Behind the steamer is the red brick **Institute of Electrical Engineers** (1886–90). To the right are the stepped blocks of the neo-Georgian **Brettenham House** (1931–2). This was the first home of the BBC. Further to the right are the spans of **Waterloo Bridge**, providing cover for the second-hand-book market on the south side of the river.

SCENE SEVENTEEN

Waterloo Bridge offers one of the finest views of the river and the brilliant effect of its white Portland stone impresses, especially in sunlight.

The original bridge was built by John Rennie as Strand Bridge and renamed following the Battle of Waterloo. This was the bridge that was depicted by Constable and painted some forty times by Monet, presumably between lunches and dinners at the Savoy. It was demolished in 1932, despite public outcry, and was replaced in 1943 by an attractive bridge to the designs of Sir Giles Gilbert Scott. The bridge made news in 1978 when Georgi Markov, a Bulgarian dissident who was working for the BBC, was stabbed while walking across it. The attack was carried out by a member of the Bulgarian secret service, who used a sharp-pointed umbrella tipped with ricin. Markov died.

To the right of this scene is the magnificent Palladian facade of **Somerset House**, the only building in London that could attempt to rival the Louvre in Paris, though hardly on the same scale. The architect of Somerset House was Sir William Chambers, who aspired to outdo the work of his rivals the Adam brothers at the Adelphi. He was born in Sweden and also designed the Pagoda in Kew Gardens. Work started in 1776, not an auspicious year for England, and continued to 1786. The building was let to the Royal Academy and Learned Societies as well as the Navy Board. Later it was occupied for many years by the Inland Revenue and Registrar General in an extension built by Sir James Pennethorne. Somerset House now contains the Courtauld Institute of Art with its superb collection of Old Masters, Impressionist and Post Impressionist paintings. It is also home to the Gilbert Collection of *objets d'art* and is an outpost of the Hermitage Museum in Saint Petersburg. Within Somerset House can be found the Admiralty restaurant and the cheaper River Terrace café. The interior court, which used to be a car park for civil servants, now displays a magical fountain. The name Somerset is derived from that of the first Duke of Somerset, Edward Seymour, ('Protector Somerset'), whose house occupied the site in the sixteenth century.

SCENE EIGHTEEN

Somerset House continues its eastern extension (1829) by Robert Smirke, and is occupied by **Kings College**.

Kings College was founded in 1829 as part of the University of London by the Duke of Wellington and the Church of England to counter the 'godless' University College in Bloomsbury.

At the river's edge is a **keystone arch** of the river entrance to Somerset House which has not been used since the Embankment was built.

The building on the right of Somerset House is **MacAdam House** (1972–5), a modern extension to Kings College in glass and concrete and designed in a mildly Brutalist style.

Behind the trees we can see up Surrey Street to a wing of **Australia House** with its copper neo-Mansard roof. At the right of this scene is **Arundel Great Court**, a bland concoction of stone bands and smoked glass, built in 1971–6 by Sir Frederick Gibberd & Partners. The riverfront is inhabited by the **Howard Hotel**.

A continuation of the Howard Hotel to the left and at its base the balustrades on the roof of **Temple Station** (1914–15), once the haunt of prostitutes.

The red-brick building on the corner is **Arundel House** (1884), occupied since 1998 by the International Institute of Strategic Studies, a think tank on political and military conflict. Arundel House was built for the Norfolk Estate and is collegiate in style with knobbly Tudor-like chimneys. Beside it, is **Globe House** (1996–8), the head-quarters of the British-American Tobacco Co., identified by its shallow imitation- copper roof. Bronze figures of Mercury at its entrance represent trade and commerce.

The white ship is **HMS Wellington**, a former sloop built in 1934. HMS *Wellington* was involved in the evacuation of Dunkirk and also served as a convoy escort in the Atlantic. In 1948 it was converted and is now the 'livery hall' of the Honourable Company of Master Mariners.

Behind HMS *Wellington* is the former Astor Estate office, designed by J.L. Pearson in 1895 in an inventive and elaborate Elizabethan style. It is now occupied by the **Bulldog Trust**, a charity. Atop the building is a beaten gilded image of the caravel *Santa Maria*, Columbus's ship.

In the distance, overshadowing the **Temple Gardens**, is the spire of G.E. Street's Gothic Revival **Law Courts** (1871–82) in the Strand, where it is said lawyers argue endlessly in stuffy Dickensian rooms. The Great Hall by contrast is a superbly organised space.

At the left is **Temple Gardens**, a white Portland stone building, Victorian, prosperous-looking and a little smug, possibly like its barrister occupants. The building is French in style.

The Temple itself is hidden by trees, but some description is called for. This collegiate oasis for lawyers, lying between busy Strand and hectic Victoria Embankment, reminds one of Oxford or Cambridge. It unfolds in a maze of courts and passageways as complex as the legal system itself. The Temple is divided into Inner Temple and Middle Temple. Why Temple? The Knights Templar, a medieval military order, took its name from the Temple in Jerusalem where they were stationed to protect Christian pilgrims. They set up house here in 1160 after being evicted by the Turks. When the Order was suppressed in 1312 the property was held by the Order of Saint John of Jerusalem.

Eventually, following the Dissolution of the Monasteries, part of the property was taken by Henry VIII for Bridewell Palace. Then in 1609, the Temple was leased by James I to the lawyers, now primarily barristers, who carry on their work and training here to this day.

A centrepiece of the Temple is the circular Temple Church, built in 1185, which, despite being bombed in World War II, still contains effigies of Templar knights, although most are restored. The Temple gardens provide the scene in Shakespeare's play *Henry VI, Part I* where the dispute between the houses of York and Lancaster begins, as decribed by the words of Warwick:

And here I prophesy: this brawl today,
Grown to this faction in the Temple garden,
Shall send between the red rose and the
white
A thousand souls to death and deadly
night.

The buff-funnelled former warship is **HMS President**. The ship was built in 1918 as HMS *Saxifrage*, a convoy-protection ship. These vessels were known as Q ships and were disguised as merchant ships and expected to destroy enemy submarines when they surfaced. HMS *President* has been moored at the Victoria Embankment for some eighty years. It is now a convention and function centre.

Scene Twenty-One

Here is a perfect frieze of buildings, like a mini Bruges or Antwerp. The Renaissance style **Hamilton House** (1898–1901) is hidden behind the trees. **Telephone House** (1898–1902), a baroque high-relief pastiche, is now home to solicitors Harcus Sinclair. **Audit House** (1903) is now the Employment Appeal Tribunal, in neo-Wren red brick and stone. **New Carmelite House** (1989–93)

attempts, in a postmodern way, to emulate its neighbours but without particular success. Next door to it is the red-brick Gothic Revival **Sion College**, once a magnificent library of 100,000 volumes and a social centre for the clergy until 1996. In the distance beyond Sion College is the arching shape of the **International Press Centre**.

Scene Twenty-Two

This scene reflects an architectural drama with the curving white **Unilever House** edging suddenly towards **Blackfriars Bridge**. On the

left is the ornate former site of the City of London School for Boys (1880–92), which was originally founded by John Carpenter in 1442.

The French neo-Renaissance style school was occupied from the 1880s but removed in 1986 to a site east of Blackfriars Bridge. It is now the offices of J.P. Morgan bankers.

Squeezed between the former School for Boys and Unilever House is the wedding cake-like spire of **St Bride's** (1701–3), a Wren church gutted in World War II and then restored.

Unilever House (1930–32) is a massive faux-Baroque design for the prestige headquarters of Unilever. Characterised by its heavy rustication at ground level and huge Ionic columns, it is embellished by energetic giant figures who are seen restraining horses as symbols of Controlled Energy. The Art-Deco interior is splendid. Unilever is one of the biggest food companies in the world and was created out of the merger of Lever Brothers and a Dutch company in the 1930s.

Blackfriars Bridge looms to the right. But why Blackfriars? The name comes from Blackfriars Monastery, which stood nearby in Blackfriars Lane from 1276 until its dissolution in 1538. The Black Friars were the Dominican Order of Preachers founded by Saint Dominic (1170–1221). The monks wore black cloaks over their habits, hence Black Friars. The remarkable Arts and Crafts **Black Friar pub** continues the Dominican theme. This was built around 1905. A statue of a laughing friar stands over the doorway.

Blackfriars Bridge was built originally in 1760–69 as Pitt Bridge. The bridge was rebuilt by Joseph Cubitt in the 1860s. Its enormous red granite columns can be seen with their leafy Portland stone capitals, said to represent pulpits. It was from Blackfriars Bridge that the body of Roberto Calvi was found hanging on 18th June 1982. Calvi, known as 'God's Banker' because of his close connections with the Vatican, was murdered, probably by the Mafia.

SCENES TWENTY-THREE AND TWENTY-FOUR

Underneath **Blackfriars Bridge** on the southern side is a walkway with depictions on its walls of the former Pitt Bridge and the erection of the Cubitt bridge.

SCENE TWENTY-FIVE

Beside Blackfriars Bridge on the left is the yellow stock brick **Bridge House**. Next door is the river frontage of Richard Seifert's **165 Queen Victoria Street**, a strongly horizontal design built between 1977 and 1987. It is now the offices of accountants KPMG. Seifert was one of the most commercially successful architects of the 1960s and 70s. He had a reputation for building to budget and on time, but the results are often mundane. Roy Porter called him 'a purveyor of conveyor-belt modernism'.

At the right of this scene are strange marching red-granite columns on a voyage to nowhere.

They are the remnants of what remains of the western bridge built by Joseph Cubitt in 1862–4 for the London Chatham and Dover Railway. Prominent pylons display the badge of LCDR. The existing railway bridge, called **St Paul's Railway Bridge**, was built in the 1880s by Thomas Wolfe Barry and H.M. Brunel. It now carries Thameslink trains.

SCENE TWENTY-SIX

Takes us underneath the railway bridge on the southern side.

SCENE TWENTY-SEVEN

The 'mute' Seifert building continues its horizontal way. Looking to the left we see the train entrance to the nondescript **Blackfriars Bridge Station**, described by Nikolaus Pevsner as 'a miserable job'.

SCENE TWENTY-EIGHT

The dull grey facade is **Mermaid House** (1977–81), a Seifert work. In front of this expanse of stone and glass is the reddish brick frontage of the former **Mermaid Theatre**.

The Mermaid Theatre was founded by Bernard Miles, character actor and producer. It was the first theatre to be built in the City since Shakespeare's time. It is now used by BBC 2 and offers conference facilities. The ochre, glum building that continues for the rest of this scene is the much unloved and Brutalist **Baynard House** (1972–79). This was built with ugly pre-cast aggregate balconies and houses British Telecom. A series of totemic heads by Richard Kindersley, called the Seven Ages of Man, adds a bizarre touch on the Upper Thames Street side. Baynard House took its name from the second Baynard's Castle, which stood here around 1275.

The spire in the left-hand view is that of **St Martin's within Ludgate** (1677–86), a Wren church. The green dome is that of the **Old Bailey**, the Central Criminal Courts. Old Bailey is named after a rampart erected here at the time of the Norman Conquest.

The green copper roof of **Faraday House** (1932–3), a major telephone exchange, occupied by British Telecom, leaps into view at the left. This mundane and uninspiring structure caused much public consternation due to its proximity to St Paul's.

The red-brown brick building and its small multi-windowed annex by the riverside is the **City of London School for Boys** (1983–6). The building was kept intentionally low to preserve the view of St Paul's.

The tower peeking over the City School for Boys is that of **St Benet's**. The church was built between 1678 and 1684, possibly by Wren or by Robert Hooke. This is a charming church in a charmless location. It became the Welsh church in 1879. Inigo Jones, the great Palladian architect, is buried here.

The towers and great dome of **St Paul's** come into view to the right. St Pauls Cathedral, the masterpiece of Sir Christopher Wren, dominates this end of the City. It was built between 1675 and 1711. It is a mixture of Classic and Baroque. The Classic is seen notably in its dome, two-tier columned facade and pediment depicting the Conversion of St Paul. The Baroque was applied later in the project by the placing of two fantastic towers at the sides. Its interior was pervaded by a cool, proportionate classicism, not unexpected from a mathematician and scientist. Christopher Wren and Horatio Nelson are buried here amongst mainly military or naval heroes. The funeral of Winston Churchill took place here as well as the wedding of Prince Charles and Lady Diana Spencer.

Millennium Bridge stretches across the left side of this scene. Designed by Norman Foster in 1999 to link the Tate Modern with St Paul's, the bridge opened in the Millennium year but unfortunately developed a wobble and had to be closed three days later. Technical problems stemming from its novel design had been underestimated. These were resolved by engineers Arup by 2002. In effect this is a depressed suspension bridge with horizontal rather than vertical suspension. This approach was adopted to achieve unrestricted views of the river and to accord with the vision that inspired Norman Foster, which was of a rope bridge across a pass in the Himalayas. At night it appears as a blade of light.

The yellow building to the left of the bridge is occupied by the **Old Mutual Insurance Company**, a South African based life assurance company. The building is a postmodern block of 1987–8, by R. Seifert and Partners, in beige stone with clumsy decoration. Next door is **Norfolk House**, a residential block of flats belonging to the same development. Above them is seen the glass vault of the enormous postmodern **Alban Gate** towers (1988–92) by Terry Farrell. The red- striped brick and glass building is **Broken Wharf**, a name dating back to the thirteenth century. Rising above it is the stainless-steel ribbed-glass skyscraper **City Point**, formerly offices of British Petroleum, now home to lawyers Simmonds and Simmonds. The building with the crane above it is the redevelopment of the **Sir John Lyon** building as residential flats. The brick, yellow and red building with the keystone arch is **Brooks Wharf** (1874). This is the last remaining true riverfront warehouse and incorporates the **Samuel Pepys pub**, which has excellent views across the river to Tate Modern.

Over the top of the buildings, on the left, you can see the brown towers and jutting balconies of the **Barbican**. Barbican is a unique residential estate named after a watchtower demolished by Henry III in 1267. It arose phoenix-like from bomb sites to the design of Chamberlain Powell and Bon between 1956 and 1981. The estate provides a dramatic mix of Brutalist concrete tower blocks and lower-level, red- brick, barrel-vaulted flats. The scheme includes the Barbican Arts Centre, the London School for Girls and the Guildhall School of Music, as well as the Museum of London. After a controversial beginning, Barbican is the prized home for well-off city workers who like convenience with a touch of grandeur. 'Not for the faint-hearted,' commented Nikolaus Pevsner.

To the left of the crane is the pointed steeple of **St Mary le Bow** (1670–80). This is a city church built by Wren after the Great Fire in 1666. It was destroyed again in World War II and largely rebuilt following the design of Wren. St Mary le Bow is the sister church to Trinity Church in Wall Street, New York. It contains a memorial to Admiral Philip, who was born nearby and who took the First Fleet to Australia in 1787.

In the right corner of this scene is the blue-green forty-one-storey **Swiss Re building** (1997–2004). This is the headquarters of the Swiss Reinsurance company, built on the site of the Baltic Exchange, which was destroyed by an IRA bomb in 1992. It is described by Norman Foster, its architect, as 'London's first ecological building'. Its dense garden spaces re-oxygenate stale air. Its aerodynamic shape reduces the effect of down draughts. A distinctive, even a beautiful building, it won Foster the Stirling Prize in 2004 and is generally known as the Gherkin. Just to the right of the Gherkin is the rounded tower of the huge postmodern-style **Broadgate** development, in which Skidmore Owings and Merrill and Arup Associates were involved.

This scene looks downriver towards **Southwark Bridge**, and further in the distance the towers of **Tower Bridge**. On the left we catch a glimpse of **Vintners Place** and its Classic Revival portico built in 1990–3. The Vintners are a livery company of wine importers. Livery companies originated as fraternities of tradesmen and craftsmen in the fourteenth and fifteenth century, providing regulation of trade and mutual help. Now they have mostly evolved into honorific and charitable societies. Many livery companies retain their Livery Halls, some surviving the Great Fire and bombing in World War II and some rebuilt.

Next are the brown triumphal twin towers of **Cannon Street Station**, built in 1865–6 for the South Eastern Railway. The towers were restored in 1986 with leaded domes and spires as if to harmonise with the Wren churches. The domes used to hold water tanks for hydraulic lifts, and up to 1958 there was an iron train shed between the towers. Nearby is the site of the Hanseatic merchants' steelyard, in use from the thirteenth to the sixteenth century.

Southwark Bridge, painted in green and yellow colours, was built in 1931 and designed by Sir Ernest George.

Immediately to the right is the walk's final destination, the **Tate Modern**, seen where the Millennium Bridge walkway brings its pedestrians to a gentle landing.

The Tate Modern and Herzog & DeMeuron have done for Southwark what the Guggenheim Museum and Frank Gehry have done for Bilbao. Tate Modern is an outstanding architectural success and a regeneration of culture in a bleak environment. Nicholas Serota was inspired to convert Sir Giles Gilbert Scott's power station and to install there the modern collection of the Tate. Herzog & DeMeuron retained the tall chimney, converted the turbine hall into a vast exhibition space and made the ramp a spacious approach to the ticket office and galleries. The building is a heroic recycling of an industrial monument and a joy to visitors.

Identified in this scene, looking down the south bank of the river, are several prominent sites. The **Globe Theatre** can be seen in front of the pedestrian way. The new Globe Theatre was built in the 1990s, by American film director Sam Wanamaker, over a former bear-baiting pit and near the site of the Elizabethan Globe Theatre. The new Globe opened in 1997 and is a theatre with galleried stalls and space for a standing audience open to the weather but very popular. Next door is the **International Shakespeare Globe Centre**. Beyond can be seen the bulging glass and steel spinnaker of **Riverside House**

(2001), which now provides offices for Ofcom, the regulator of the communications industry. Further in the distance is the multi-windowed **No 1 London Bridge** (1986), a building worthy of New York, with its slick finish and imaginative use of space.

Further beyond may yet arise London Bridge Tower, or the 'Glass Shard', designed by Renzo Piano, the co-designer with Richard Rogers of the Pompidou Centre in Paris. Renzo Piano envisages a slender spire-like tower, which is planned to be the tallest building in Europe and to replace the dreary 1970s office block next to London Bridge Station. Plans include the addition of a new hotel, public piazza and bus station.

SCENE THIRTY-TWO

The final scene shows the piazza at the entrance of Tate Modern and in the distance, to the right, the curious yellow **Bankside Lofts** (1998), designed by CZMW, an eccentric and successful architectural practice. There are 130 apartments here with offices and a café in a muted postmodern style.

Simon Bradley and Nikolaus Pevsner: *The Buildings of England : London 1 : City of London*

Bridget Cherry and Nikolaus Pevsner: *The Buildings of England : London 2 : South*

Simon Bradley and Nikolaus Pevsner: *The Buildings of England : London 6 : Westminster*

Ed Glinert: *The London Compendium*

Edward Jones and Christopher Woodward: *A Guide to the Architecture of London*

Ian Nairn: *Nairn's London*

Kenneth Powell: *New London Architecture*

Roy Porter: *London: A Social History*

Ken Allinson: *London's Contemporary Architecture*

Ed Gilnert: *Literary London*

Samantha Hardingham: *London*

BIG thank you to Brian & Cecilia Parker.
David, Penny, Michael & Madeleine Penton.
Monique & Staffan Tollgard. Mr Alex Dunlop &
Mary Wadsworth. Russel.D at BS/ Mike.H at W.
Henrik Lindvall, Dan & Tim, everyone else
and anyone who Built, or Lives in
LONDON.